Mindful Musings & Peaceful Ponderings

Manali Desai

Ukiyoto Publishing

All global publishing rights are held by

Ukiyoto Publishing

Published in 2023

Content Copyright © Manali Desai
ISBN 9789360168421

All rights reserved.

No part of this publication may be reproduced, transmitted, or stored in a retrieval system, in any form by any means, electronic, mechanical, photocopying, recording or otherwise, without the prior permission of the publisher.

The moral rights of the author have been asserted.

This is a work of fiction. Names, characters, businesses, places, events, locales, and incidents are either the products of the author's imagination or used in a fictitious manner. Any resemblance to actual persons, living or dead, or actual events is purely coincidental.

This book is sold subject to the condition that it shall not by way of trade or otherwise, be lent, resold, hired out or otherwise circulated, without the publisher's prior consent, in any form of binding or cover other than that in which it is published.

www.ukiyoto.com

Dedication

Dear Husband,

You and I are,
JoMo together, FoMo when far
We flicker alone, with each other, shine
Now even my dedications rhyme
When will you for reading my books, get in line?

P.S: Me – 6, You - 0

Contents

Just A Call Away	1
Full Circle	2
Lost Identity	4
Home Sweet Home	6
Mirror, Mirror On The Wall	7
Homecoming	8
My Bad	9
Sorry Not Sorry	11
Hello, Old Friend	12
Never Gone	14
Such A Boring Life	15
What To Do, What Not To Do	16
You Can, You Must, You Will	17
Take A Break, Don't Break	18
Breaking The Norms	19
M For Mischief	20
Scarred For Life	22
Becoming Undeserving	23
Moments Of Joy	24
Some Are Like That	26
Mood-i	27
The Making Of Success	28
Sometimes Easy, Sometimes Tough	29
Celebrations	31
Mind Vs Body	33
What Happened Then?	34
Follow, Unfollow	35
Instability, Uncertainty, Unsurety	37

It's Okay To Not Try	38
Don't Stop, Make It Pop	39
Slow Motion, Potion	40
Relentless	41
Different ≠ Wrong	42
Not A Regular	43
Give And Take	44
Closer Than They Appear	46
The Great Fall	47
Say 'Me…..'	48
A Tense Meeting	49
No Trespassing	50
Not In So Many Words	51
Not My Precious	53
Was I Wrong	54
The Feeling Is Mutual	56
Strength, Not Strong	58
A Better Future	59
Where I Was, Where I Am	62
Lost At First Sight	64
It Might Just Come True	66
Can You Help Me Understand?	67
About the Author	75

Just A Call Away

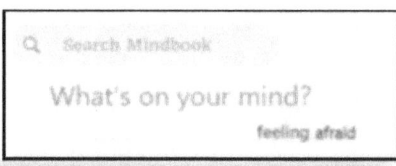

A phone ring cracked the silence of the room
She picked up
It was the call she had been waiting for
It was from the one she loved the most
The expressions changed from frowns to smiles
A relief on realizing all was well
The mother wasn't afraid anymore

A feeling of being watched and followed
She quickened her footsteps
All the while watching over her shoulder
She ran the last few steps
Heaving a sigh of relief she called the person who had helped her calm down
It was the one she relied on for everything
It was the one without whom she felt lost
The expressions changed from fear to relief
A smile spread across her face
The daughter wasn't afraid anymore

Full Circle

At 3

I felt it when my mother said, "You won't be the only child in the family now."

Because I wasn't prepared to have my parents' love divided
At 7

I felt it when my father said, "You are elder to him. Learn to give him more."
When I didn't let my brother play with my toys

At 11

I felt it when my teacher said, "You need more practice. I can't let you participate."

Because I knew she had done the selection based on favouritism
At 17,

I felt it when a girl in my class said, "You? No way! I'd rather kiss a frog."
When I was just looking for friendship

At 21,

I felt it when the interviewer said, "If only you had performed better in the written test, we would have hired you."

Because I had aced the other rounds and my cumulative score was superior to most

At 25,

I felt it when my girlfriend said, "I really like you. But I can't tolerate your parents and your little brother."

When her own family was snooty and had far bigger issues At 28,

I felt it when my wife said, "You are not as successful as your friends. I don't know what I saw in you."

Because we were at an office party surrounded by my colleagues, and she didn't mean it as a joke

At 33,

I felt it when my son said, "I don't want to have a brother or sister." When I realized life had come full circle

I knew then that what I had felt most of my life was something I could let go of

And just like that my anger was replaced with acceptance

Lost Identity

I gave up my dream job
To take care of the family
To maintain the household
To look after everyone's needs; his, the parents and then the kids
To constantly at the beck and call of everyone
To try and make my husband understand why I am unhappy, and failing all the time
What did he do for me?
I don't know for how long I can keep doing this

I gave up the girl I loved
To fulfil my family's wish of getting married to the girl of their choice
To spend my life with a girl I hardly knew
To see my wife's dissatisfied face every day
To become a father when I didn't even want a child
To keep trying to make everyone happy, and failing all the time
What am I getting in return?
I don't know for how long I can keep doing this

On our 5th wedding anniversary
He left for work without even wishing me
The others didn't acknowledge the milestone too
I didn't want to remember the day much either
So I went on with the day, just like normal
The feeling of being unloved, unappreciated, a bit escalated
"I'll show them all tonight. Enough is enough." I decided
My bitter thoughts now turned into determination
To stand up for myself, to get back my identity

It's been five years today

She believes I have forgotten such a big milestone
It was hard but I ignored her hurtful looks as I left the house
The others too were behaving aloof
I wanted to remember this day forever, for her and myself
So I left from work early, unlike normal
The feeling of wanting to show we all cared, a new one
"I'll show her today. Enough is enough." I had decided
My bitter thoughts now turned into determination
To help her to something of her own, to support her in getting back her identity

Home Sweet Home

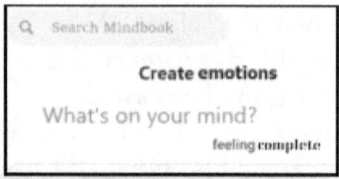

Home,
Where you can speak,
Unfiltered
Home,
Where your heart beats,
Uninhibited.
Home,
Where your smile is,
Unrestrained
Home,
Where your freedom is,
Unchained
Home,
Where your happiness is,
Unbound
Home,
Rarely, a place
Home,
Sometimes, a person
Home
Mostly, a feeling, of being complete
Home,
Never confined.
Home,
By all, uniquely defined.

Mirror, Mirror On The Wall

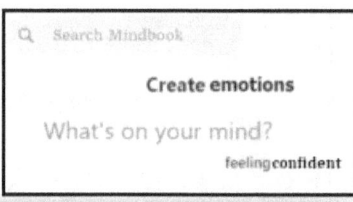

I looked at the mirror, assuring myself, "You look great!" And stepped out of my room brimming with self-confidence. Mother said, *"That color doesn't go well with your skin tone"* "But I like it and I think I look great!"

I stepped out of my house, happy with my choice, albeit with a little dent in my confidence.

The neighbor said, *"That outfit is a little tight, isn't it? You should wear loose-fitting clothes for your body type."*

"I know what suits my body type and this outfit fits well." I made my way to work, the dent in my confidence a little bigger. A colleague asked, *"Doesn't wearing a sleeveless blouse to work, make you feel self-conscious about your flabby arms?"* "It is what it is."

The confidence was now nowhere in sight as self-doubt slowly replaced self-assurance.

I asked the mirror, "Do I really look great?"

The reflection stared back confused and sorrowful.

As I took in my size, shape, and color, I asked again, "Does this define me?"

The reflection smiled and said, "Yes, it does. And yes, you look great with it all."

Just like that, the self-assurance dominated the self-doubt again.

Homecoming

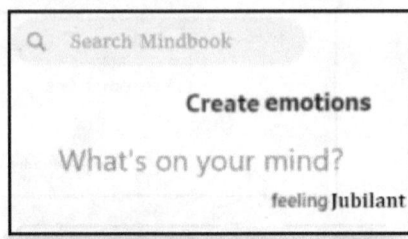

Homecoming, rejoicing
An arrival after ages,
Mind, body, heart, and soul, all eagerly awaiting.

With stars in tearful eyes,
That matched those on his uniform,
The sacrifice worth the pride.

A hero returns,
A family rejoices,
A nation secured

My Bad

> Q Search Mindbook
>
> **Create emotions**
>
> What's on your mind?
>
> feeling apologetic

When it was their turn

They said, "You are not good enough"
I understood, "I'm a failure"
So I gave up and apologized
Maybe I was the bad one

They said, "Let's do something new"
I understood, "I don't like your company"
So I apologized and let them be
Maybe I was the bad one

They said, "You've changed"
I understood, "I don't like you anymore"
So I apologized and adjusted myself to their liking
Maybe I was the bad one

Then one day,
They stopped saying anything at all

When it was my turn

I said, "You can do better"
They understood, "You are not good enough"
My bad I guess
So I apologized because I felt sorry

I meant, "Let's do something new"
They understood, "I am bored with you"
My bad I guess
So I apologized because I felt sorry

I said, "I like you more now"
They understood, "I hated you before"
My bad I guess
So I apologized because I felt sorry

I said, "You looked better in that dress"
They understood, "You are ugly whatever you wear and do"
My bad I guess
So I apologized because I felt sorry

Am I bad then?
Or is it my bad?

Sorry Not Sorry

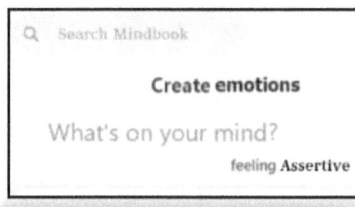

I said,
"No, you may not"
To your request, rather a demand.
I said,
"No, I'm not comfortable"
To your query on whether I'd like to join you and a few others.
I said,
"I can't do it"

To your ask for help and advice.
All the questions and my responses,
Expected me to be apologetic,
About being unavailable,
About being assertive in my refusal,
About putting myself and my comfort first.

But I refuse, to be so.
And, with pleasure,
I just want to say,
Sorry, not sorry.

Hello, Old Friend

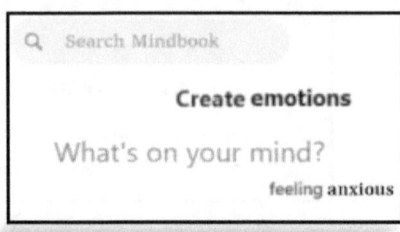

We haven't properly met,
Since that time, I managed to speak about myself through trembling speech and body, in front of my batchmates.

But you do show up every now and then,

Like yesterday when someone asked me, *"Do you consider yourself successful?"*

And I hesitated just a bit before going on to explain what success means to me.

Or that day a few months ago,
When someone said, *"I don't believe people are paying you for this!"*
And I felt a blow to my ego but quickly recovered as I reminded myself that one person's opinion didn't matter.

I also faintly recall,
You popping up in between my deadlines and ongoing tasks, making me doubt if I'll be able to deliver.

But I'm too focused and stubborn now,
to let you deter me from my goal.

Do I miss you?

No, because you're still very much there.

We have been friends for too long,
My dear **Mr. Anxiety**.

But it has been a while for sure!
Because you are in me and a part of me.

However, your nemesis, **Mr. Self-confidence,**
Is doing just a tad better lately.

Never Gone

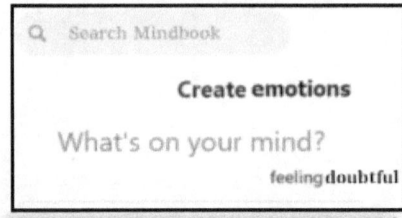

In thoughts,
In movements,

In the form of doubts about self,
In the form of suspicion on and about others,

Through words,
Spoken and mostly unspoken.

Through actions,
Sometimes done,
Generally, undone.

Almost always there,
Making all and sundry,
Unsure, uncertain.

Only sometimes absent.
When not,
Assured confidence,
And a positive outcome.

People call it anxiety
Some, nervousness
I call it, a necessary evil that's never gone

Such A Boring Life

> Search Mindbook
>
> **Create emotions**
>
> What's on your mind?
>
> feeling **bored**

Mistaken for laziness,
Sometimes also for indifference,
Maybe even drowsiness,
But the thing is,
They're mere by-products
of an emotion,
widely experienced,
But never clearly understood.
Lurking in bodies and minds,
it shows up when an activity or a person,
seems uninteresting.

Like someone talking and talking without listening,
or an act that involves work we don't want to engage in.
Like, maybe something you're feeling right now too?
Like, something we often refer to as, "Such a boring life"
or, "This is so boring"
and our most favourite , "I'm so bored"

What To Do, What Not To Do

> Q Search Mindbook
>
> **Create emotions**
>
> What's on your mind?
>
> feeling**confused**

This or that?
Now or later?
To do or not to do?
Good or bad?
Right or wrong?
Decisions to make,
At every stage
On every occasion.
Life makes it difficult,
Our minds further complicate it.
How?
Because of this emotion called 'confusion'.
How to deal with it?
Well, that's another issue,
Because you see,
It's a life-learning process with no ensured tips or tricks,
And only experience makes it easier to deal with.

You Can, You Must, You Will

> Q Search Mindbook
>
> **Create emotions**
>
> What's on your mind?
>
> feeling**discouraged**

"Can you do it?"
"Are you sure about this?"
"You should try something else"
"You tried and failed already, just give up now maybe"
The kind of statements and questions one hears when trying something,
Especially something new.
Fuelled by the words of people around,
And probably our own past experiences too.
Making us doubt ourselves.
Sounds familiar?
Yes, that's what being discouraged is.
The best solution is to trudge on nonetheless,
With the intention
To prove to yourself more than anyone else that you can do it.
With the motivation
To become better than you were before you started off.
With the intent
To learn and grow rather than the end result of success or glory.

Take A Break, Don't Break

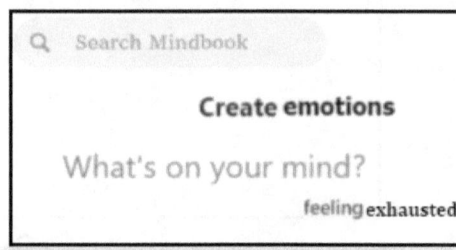

"I can't do this anymore"
"I need a break"
"My mind is numb"
"My body pains"
"My head hurts"

Different forms of saying,
All signs which show,
That you are **exhausted**,
That you can't do it anymore.
They're signals from your body and mind,
Asking you to take some rest,
From the task at hand,
Whether it is something you love or something you don't enjoy doing,
Sometimes physical, sometimes mental, quite a few times emotional too.
Doesn't matter who or what caused it.
The only thing that needs attention,
is getting rid of what's causing it.
Permanently if it's something you dislike, and if possible.
And at least for a while, if it's something you want and wish to get back to.

Breaking The Norms

> Search Mindbook
> **Create emotions**
> What's on your mind?
> feelingguilty

Going against the tide or set norms
Under pressure for having done something wrong
Inhibited about the outcome of an action
Lying, cheating, stealing, includes all sorts of deeds
Though not necessarily always fallacious
You end up feeling bad about what you've done

M For Mischief

> Search Mindbook
>
> **Create emotions**
>
> What's on your mind?
>
> feeling mischievious

Ask for the out of ordinary
Ask for the absurd
Absurd for the ordinary
Absurd for your kicks
Kicks the soul
Kicks that make you laugh
Laugh out loud
Laugh alone or with others
Others might not enjoy
Others do not matter
Matter of your happiness
Matter that satisfies
Satisfies once in a while
Satisfies the curious mind
Mind that feels
Mind that wants novelty
Novelty in words
Novelty in action
Action defiant
Action playful
Playful demeanour
Playful words
Words that make smiles
Words that create joy
Joy sometimes
Joy not for all
All do not understand

All unacceptable
Unacceptable to boring
Unacceptable for sticklers
Sticklers for obedience
Sticklers of norms
Norms mean rules
Norms lead to dullness
Dullness sadness
Dullness less happy moments
Moments to create memories
Moments to enjoy
Enjoy life
Enjoy like a child
Child-like innocence
Child-like curiosity
Curiosity to learn
Curiosity to try
Try something new
Try never done
Done for some laughter
Done to bring joy
Joy
Laughter

Scarred For Life

> 🔍 Search Mindbook
>
> **Create emotions**
>
> What's on your mind?
>
> feeling **hurt**

A scar on the face,
Big, ugly, and visible.
It made people notice and ask.
Some with concern,
some with curiosity and gossip.

"Are you alright?"
"Does it hurt?"
"What happened?"

Over time, it healed, and the pain was gone.
But, something remained.
What caused the pain,
The person who caused it,
The words that led to it,
The actions that came before and after it.
That continued to give her a scar,
That got bigger day by day.
Yet, sadly, nobody noticed,
Neither asked out of concern,
nor for mere gossip.

Becoming Undeserving

> Search Mindbook
>
> **Create emotions**
>
> What's on your mind?
>
> feeling unworthy

A bad experience,
Makes you scared of being hurt again,
You have many doubts
And innumerable questions
You're afraid of losing something or someone
It makes you vulnerable
It shows as a sign of your weakness
It makes you undesirable, unwanted
You're worried about becoming undeserving
For others, for the self

*Check out a video rendition of this poem on Instagram.com/arusticmind_*

Moments Of Joy

> Search Mindbook
>
> **Create emotions**
>
> What's on your mind?
>
> feeling Joyful

A few sources of joy
Bucket full of popcorn with your favourite movie
Catching up with an old friend
Discovering a new place
Endings that turn out better than you expected
Finding money in the pocket of your trousers
Going out for a walk on a sunny day in winters
Homecoming after a long gap
In the arms of a loved one
Joking or goofing around with your friends
Late night conversations
Managing to survive a bad experience
Not giving up on a long-desired goal
Opening up to someone
Politeness from a stranger
Quiet comfort after a chaotic day
Raindrops after a heatwave and the following smell of wet soil
Singing along to your favourite song with someone
Teaching someone something and them thanking you for the success
Unpacking a box of goodies or a gift
Visiting a place on your bucket list
Waking up without an alarm clock
Xi (admire) the little things in life
Yummy food
Zoning out of work and responsibilities.

Some Are Like That

> **Search Mindbook**
> **Create emotions**
> What's on your mind?
> feeling charitable

Some are like that,
They give, without taking.
Some are like that,
They smile, without knowing you too.
Some are like that,
They ask out of concern, without any malice.
Some are like that,
They put others first, without thinking about themselves.
Some are like that,
They feel happy about others' happiness and success, without envy.
Some are like that,
They help those in need, without anybody asking them to.
Some are like that,
They want to make the world a better place, without thinking, "What's my benefit in that?"
Some are like that,
They choose kindness first every time, without even knowing its definition.

*Check out a video rendition of this poem on Instagram.com/arusticmind_*

Mood-i

> Search Mindbook
>
> **Create emotions**
>
> What's on your mind?
>
> feeling lazy

Wanted to do a lot of things
Ended up doing a few
Because the mood was such
I didn't want to move

Ended up doing few
Tasks that begged for attention
Didn't want to move anymore
Just didn't feel like it

The body and mind didn't feel like it
Blissful ignorance of
The tasks begging for attention
As an emotion took over

The emotion took over
As hands and legs refused to move
The body and mind went along and ignored
Everything else

Hands and legs refused
To do a lot of things
So everything else stayed as it was
The mood was such

The Making Of Success

> Q Search Mindbook
>
> **Create emotions**
>
> What's on your mind?
>
> feeling nervous

On the precipice of something new,
A big day, a good performance, expected, needed

Many faces, few known, most alien,
The matter, familiar, yet lack of confidence

Body shivering, heart fluttering
Fear, of failure, of unacceptance, of ridicule

A mass familiar scenario,
The result? Someone's success story in the making

Sometimes Easy, Sometimes Tough

> Q Search Mindbook
>
> **Create emotions**
>
> What's on your mind?
>
> feeling optimistic

When **life is tough**
Thinking of what you have
Instead of what you don't
Recalling the happy days
Remembering that this is just a phase

There will be bad and good days
Because **life is tough**
and not always easy
But there's that feeling that
helps you stay positive

Choosing to abate the negative
Accepting the struggles and challenges
When **life is tough**
Choosing to grow
Learning from it all

Life is what makes you
It is all also what you make of it
Sometimes life is easy
Sometimes **life is tough**
Never apart, all a package

Pessimists are always unhappy
The other type, those who accept,
Those who don't grumble,

They understand optimism
Because they know that **life is tough**

Celebrations

> Search Mindbook
>
> **Create emotions**
>
> What's on your mind?
>
> **feeling proud**

Tried, and failed,
Maybe it was the first attempt,
Maybe it wasn't
Most stop after that attempt
When the result does not match the expectations
When failing again is not desired

It's not necessary to be happy only when you succeed, celebrate the failures too

Success is desired by one and all,
But most want it the easy one,
Without working for it,
Without working at all.
But that's not how it works,
Because trying is involved, and sometimes failing is important too.

It's not necessary to be happy only when you succeed, celebrate the failures too

Those that keep trying
Understand where they're going wrong.
They work on improving and being better.
That's how they get the desired results.
That's what leads to more happiness than instant success.
That's what makes them proud, that's what makes others proud of them too.

It's not necessary to be happy only when you succeed, celebrate the failures too

Mind Vs Body

> Search Mindbook
>
> **Create emotions**
>
> What's on your mind?
> **feeling queasy**

Taking the ride is exciting and scary
What if your stomach misbehaves
What if, to the journey, it caves?
Taking the ride is exciting and scary

What if your stomach misbehaves?
Then you can't enjoy the ride and the views,
That's when settles in, the blues
What if your stomach misbehaves?

Then you can't enjoy the ride and the views.
Maybe you should have avoided that last bite,
The mind grumbles, over the body's plight.
Then you can't enjoy the ride and the views

Maybe you should have avoided that last bite.
When taking on something new,
Most things turn out not what you knew.
Maybe you should have avoided that last bite.

Taking the ride is exciting and scary
What if your stomach misbehaves
What if, to the journey, it caves?
Taking the first ride is exciting and scary

What Happened Then?

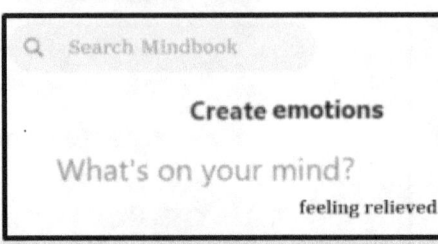

Something that's been awaited for long,
An experience in queue,
There's hope of action and result,
You feel rising curiosity,
The suspense heightens with each passing second,
What happens? Will it happen?
The desire for a good end is strong
The emotion one feels on conclusion,
Is remembered, lifelong

Follow, Unfollow

> 🔍 Search Mindbook
>
> **Create emotions**
>
> What's on your mind?
>
> feeling empathic

Zest for life may not be the same in everyone
You are no one to question or judge
Xenophobia is quite a common practice, but
Who are we to say what is right or wrong?
Victory and even failure are deserved by all
Universe is quite big, then why not our minds and thoughts?
Those who have a life different from ours are never easily liked or accepted
Should this not be a matter of concern?
Remind yourself to be kind, above everything else
Quota of love, success, and everything good in life, should it not be for all?
Perhaps we need to learn some new ways of life and unlearn the redundant ones
Or maybe, just be open to people who are unlike us
No one's circumstances are what we presume or understand them to be
Most people just want to be
Let them be then, what's so difficult in that?
Kids and adults alike, all have their differences and similarities
Just try to understand each one's position and perspective
In the end, we all just want peace
Here's how we can achieve it
Going out of the way is also not required
Friends and strangers,
Embrace and accept them all

Do you know what this is?
Caring, sharing, giving, all of it, yes
But more than that
An emotion we know of but hardly ever understand and practice,
it's **EMPATHY**.

Instability, Uncertainty, Unsurety

> Search Mindbook
>
> **Create emotions**
>
> What's on your mind?
>
> feeling tensed

Instability, uncertainty, no clarity,
About the now and later,
About life going helter-skelter
All actions and decisions lay in obscurity
Instability, uncertainty, no clarity

There's confusion, there's dread,
Holding life together with a thread
In you, among others, there's insecurity
Causing instability, uncertainty, no clarity

The feeling that all will be lost
Your success, your possessions, everything, will be tossed
It's called being tensed that happens in moments of severity,
Leading to instability, uncertainty, no clarity

It's Okay To Not Try

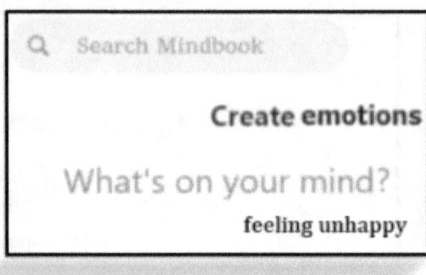

When you are not able to smile,
If you find it difficult to be happy,
When joy hasn't visited you in a while
If everything that happens around makes you snappy
When the world seems cruel and unfair
If others' success and happiness make you question your worth
When all and everyone become too much to bear
If, of unfortunate and unpleasant events, seems to be no dearth
What you're going through is not bizarre,
The way you feel is also an emotion, albeit crappy
It might even leave a scar
It does have a name, called 'unhappy'

So, it is okay to frown,
It is okay to cry,
It is okay to feel down,
It is okay for a while, to not try.

Don't Stop, Make It Pop

> Q Search Mindbook
>
> **Create emotions**
>
> What's on your mind?
>
> **feeling victorious**

Sometimes I,
At times, we
Many try,
Leads to glee

Fail, don't mind
Never stop
Life, a grind
Pause, don't drop

Win, a few,
Loss, some more
All are due
Upward soar

Slow Motion, Potion

> Search Mindbook
>
> **Create emotions**
>
> What's on your mind?
>
> **feeling worried**

Here lies an emotion,
That's long deserved this demotion.
It caused many a commotion,
Anxiety, unrest, panic, all its notion.
Let us remember it as a potion,
That led us to success in slow motion.

Relentless

> Search Mindbook
>
> **Create emotions**
>
> What's on your mind?
> feeling motivated

Why do we want what we don't have?
What is it about the unreachable that attracts us?
When does the desire for more stop?

The answer is….NEVER
Because that's what motivation is

We grow with the want,
The unreachable helps us work harder
The desire fuels our ambition.

*Check out a video rendition of this poem on Instagram.com/arusticmind_*

Different ≠ Wrong

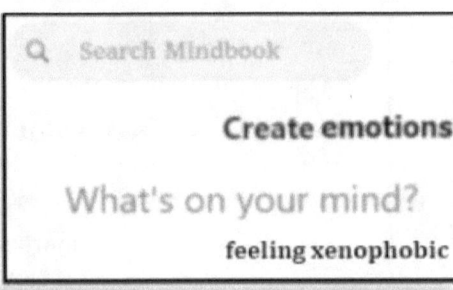

Unusual, against the norm
Like a freeform
Wants acceptance
Gets susceptance

Stereotypes, misogyny,
Synonymy
Majority
Otherity

Of the alien, unaccepting
Intercepting
Detrimental
Judgemental

Note: *The word 'otherity' used in the poem is a self-constructed verb derived from the noun 'other' meaning a person or group of people intrinsically different from and alien to oneself.*

Not A Regular

> Search Mindbook
>
> **Create emotions**
>
> What's on your mind?
>
> feeling quirky

Quirky, fun, lively
Sentiment
Not a regular

Spreading laughter,
Causing curiosity
Making a statement

An awareness
A something that sets apart
The regular from the not-so-common

Give And Take

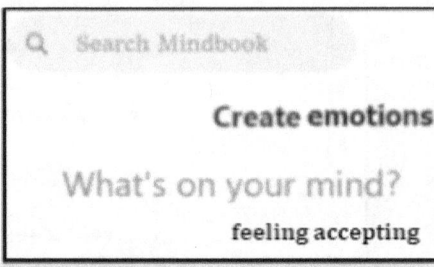

Most believe,
Some don't,
Most get it,
Others crave for it,
Each with their own definition,
Each with their experience,
Each with their own expectations,
Some, happy with what they have,
Many wanting more than what comes their way,
The one feeling that binds us all,
Why is it limited to a 'couple'?
Is it not the same,
with family,
friends,
and everyone we care about?
Is it not love?
When we choose someone else before us?
Even if not our 'better half' or our 'significant other'?
Then why this question,

on everyone's mind,

about,

To love or not to love?
Why can we not
Choose to follow the popular mantra of
Give and Take
For something we all crave for the most

Closer Than They Appear

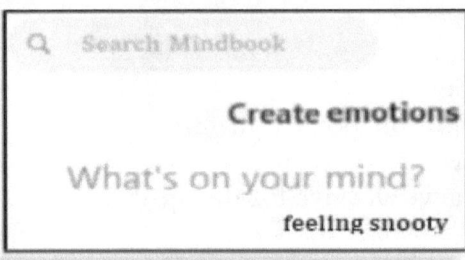

He spoke,
But hardly ever listened
She judged
But did not like being told off
He promised
But never delivered
Do they sound familiar?
Focused on the self
Not caring who gets affected by their words and actions
Wanting only the best
Not bothering about how it came about
Pitying the lesser fortunate
Not wanting to extend even a little help or even a word of kindness
Attracted to beauty
But only the kind that pleased the eye
Richness exuding from their style
Pockets generally full of wealth
Who are they?
People we find unattractive
Because they are
What we deny being
But also,
A reflection of our ugly sides
And they're
You and me,
On most or some days.

The Great Fall

> Search Mindbook
>
> **Create emotions**
>
> What's on your mind?
>
> **feeling desolate**

Standing on the edge,
It was a risk worth taking.
Taking a deep breath, he thought to himself,
'At least I won't regret not trying it.'
Looking down at the depth of the fall,
He reminded himself,
'I might hurt myself with the experience of it,
But maybe the scars will help convince people,
That I am indeed in pain,
And finally, they will see the proof,
That my emotional scars failed to show.'

Say 'Me…..'

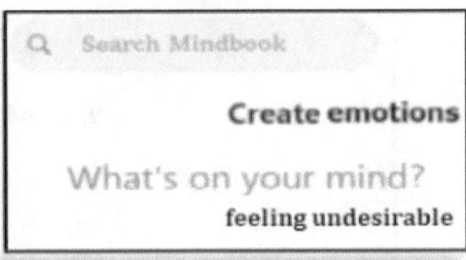

Who cares?

Those that brought you into this world do, your parents.

Who cares?

The one who has vowed to stand by you does, your partner.

Who cares?

The ones you grew up with do, your siblings.

Who cares?

The ones who held your hand in good and bad times do, your friends.

Who cares?

The ones who respect you for your work and achievements do, your admirers.

Who cares?

The person you were yesterday and have grown into today, does, yourself.

Who cares?

The one in the mirror does, the reflection of your strength and survival.

A Tense Meeting

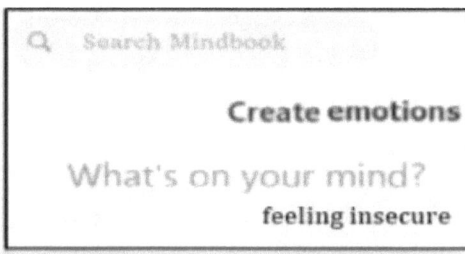

A mistake from the past
Haunting the present
Something done in an impulse
Something that happened eons back
Something that was buried in the back lanes of memory
Something you believed was done and dusted with
Something you have regretted every day since it happened and ended

But now it's back
It's back in a manner you'd never imagined
It's back in a way worse than before
It's back such that you're threatened

What if you lose all those you care for?
What if it breaks you in a manner that you're never the same again?
What if, everything you've worked so hard for, becomes immaterial because of that one thing?

That one mistake from the past
That refuses to be blocked out

No Trespassing

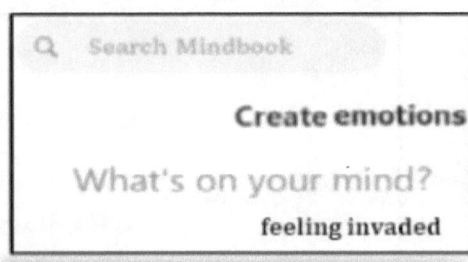

It is likely that somebody crossed a line,

Many eons ago,

Before privacy and personal space,

were clearly defined.

Probably someone thought out loud or in their mind,

"Hey, I don't like you being so close to me."

Or

"I wish there was a way to stop people from entering a certain space I can call my own."

Or

"Can there be a way to shut people out?"

Or

"Should we have a system where people need to ask for permission before coming too close?"

And maybe that's why we have doors.

Both physical and emotional.

Not In So Many Words

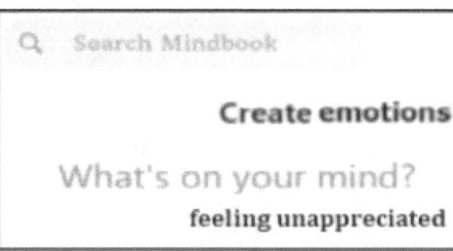

He didn't show how much
She thought he did not
Was the care missing then?

She wanted flowers, chocolates, and diamonds,
He gave support, respect, and time instead
Was it lesser of a gift then?

He never said, 'You're beautiful the way you are'
She thought it meant, 'You're ugly'
Did it invalidate what he thought of her then?

She wanted dinner outings and walks on the beach
He took her out but did not want to bother her with the where, how and when
Did it make it less of a date then?

When she got sick, he never asked, "How're you feeling?" But silently took over all her responsibilities
When he got sick, she would constantly ask, "What can I get for you?" and he would up and about in a few days
Does that mean one does more for the other in comparison then?

Their child got into trouble one day
She said, "Be more like you father" and he said "Be more like your

mother"
Does that count as validation of their feelings for each other then?

She looked at him in surprise
He looked at her in admiration
Both wondering, does love always need to be verbal?

Not My Precious

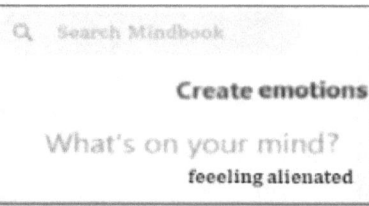

Daddy's little girl,
Mommy's princess
Everyone's precious doll
She believed the world existed only for her

Until she stepped out and became
Mostly a nobody
Usually a somebody
On most days ignored by everybody
On some days not accepted by anybody

Reality hit
Privilege now equality
Arrogance replaced by humility
Definition of needs a little different

Hard
But not impossible
Tough
But survivable

Life happened
Blessing in disguise maybe
A wake up call
Needed for all

Was I Wrong

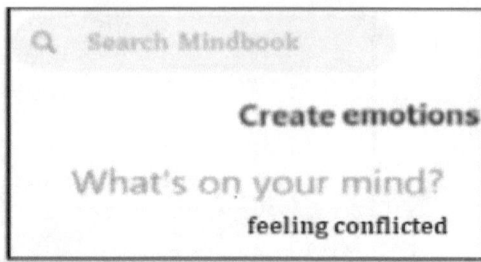

I replied, "I don't know"
When my teacher asked, "Who threw this chalk at me?"
Instead of answering, "My friend did it."
Was I wrong in doing so?

I said, "It's the girl next door"
When my father asked, "Who is your sister talking to?"
Instead of answering, "She is talking to a boy she likes."
Was I wrong in doing so?

I answered, "It was a team effort"
When my boss asked, "Well done. How did you arrive at this result?"
Instead of saying, "I did most of the leg work"
Was I wrong in doing so?

I retorted, "You don't make time for us"
When my girlfriend said, "We hardly spend time together"
Instead of saying, "I'm sorry. I will try to be a better boyfriend from now on"
Was I wrong in doing so?

I responded with, "I reached on time"
When my team members arrived a little late and asked, "What time did you get here?"
Instead of saying, "I was late too. Don't worry"
Was I wrong in doing so?

I countered with, "Everyone does it"
Whenever someone said, "Please don't litter"

Instead of saying, "I am sorry. Let me throw that in the dustbin"
Was I wrong in doing so?

Every time I felt conflicted
I chose the easy way out
Instead of the right way
Was I wrong in doing so?

Today, I stand with the consequences
Still mostly choosing myself
Sometimes others with me
Am I wrong in doing so?

The Feeling Is Mutual

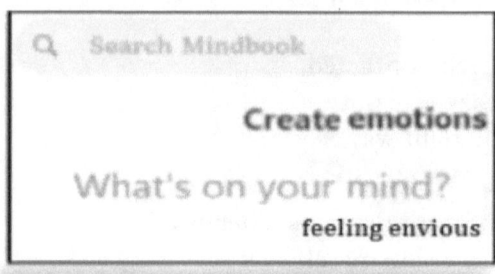

She had a fulfilling personal life

Taking care of the family and her home
Her days were filled with laughter and warmth
But a part of her always felt envious
Of the other one, who was breaking barriers at work

She had a job that she loved

Meeting deadlines, keeping her team on toes
Her days were filled with challenges and adrenaline
But a part of her always felt envious
Of the other one, who was able to give all her time to the family

He had a 9*5 desk job
That he enjoyed on most days
There was stable income that took care of all financial responsibilities

But a part of him always felt envious
Of the other one, who was not tied down with family burdens and was able to follow his passion

He travelled around the world
Chasing stories and meeting up people of different races, communities, and religions

He earned well and hardly worried about the lack of regular financial inflow
But a part of him always envious
Of the other one, who had a family that he looked forward to returning to, after a hard day at work

That feeling of missing out and wondering what life could have been
Is mutual for everyone
Because, no matter how hard we try
There's always going to be something we must forego of

Strength, Not Strong

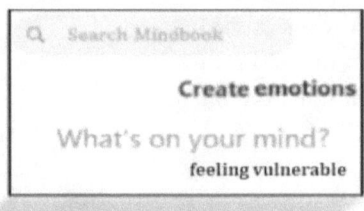

"Be brave"
"You gotta be strong"
"Learn to live with it"
"It happens to everyone"

But
What if?
You want to be a little afraid
You can't help but be weak
You just can't seem to learn how to live with it
You want to know why it happened to you

Is hiding your emotions, a sign of bravery?
Is dealing with your problems alone, an achievement?

Let's get one thing straight then
IT IS NOT

Being vulnerable does not make you weak
Strength is in admitting you need help
Strength is in accepting you are not, and cannot be, strong always

A Better Future

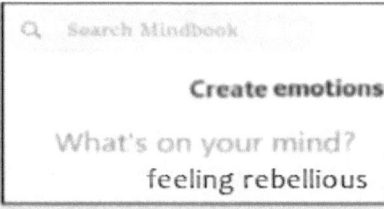

It wasn't a perfect relationship
She was told she's a burden
She was told she's not good enough
She was put down in private and public
She was made to suffer, emotional as well as physical pain
She was given scars,
Some that healed
But showed up again, every now and then
Some that didn't show
But never healed, neither now, nor ever.

But she stayed
Because society said, *"A woman must accept her husband with his flaws"*
So, she believed, that's the way it is
Because her parents said, *"Think of our reputation. What will people say if you leave your in-laws house?"*
So, she didn't know how to get out of it
Because nobody ever said, *"Do something for yourself"* or *"Have an identity of your own"*
So, if not a wife and a daughter-in-law, what and who would she be?

She then became a mother,
To a girl, a daughter,
A reflection of her
Who made her days a little brighter
But the nightmares of her life, worse
She had failed to provide a *खानदान का चिराग** after all

She had failed, as a wife, as a woman

Still, she stayed,
Because society said, *"How will you raise your child?"*
So, she bore her dark present, for her daughter's bright future
Because her parents said, *"You can try again"*
So, she let herself continue to be toyed, in the hopes of a boy, a son.

But,
There was no son,
Her misery continued to worsen
The daughter slowly grew
Witnessing it all
The mistreatment
The abuse
The craving and the demands, for another baby, unlike her
Her little mind believed it
To be normal
To be acceptable
To be a form of love

Years went by,
The daughter, now almost a woman
Who would soon be
A wife,
A daughter-in-law
And like her mother,
A mother someday herself
In apprehension of it all, the daughter asked, *"Must a woman must accept her husband with his flaws?"*
The mother knew then,
That she couldn't let her daughter believe this to be true
That her daughter cannot, should not and will not be told, *"Think of the family's reputation"*
So, she said, *"Do something for yourself and have an identity of your own"*
She was determined for her daughter to be
More than herself
More than somebody's wife

More than someone's daughter-in-law
More than a mother
And definitely more than
Just another woman
She wanted her daughter to have
A life, unlike hers
A past and present, different from hers
A future,
Better than women like her.

खानदान का चिराग = *A mail heir considered to take the family's reputation and lineage ahead.*

Where I Was, Where I Am

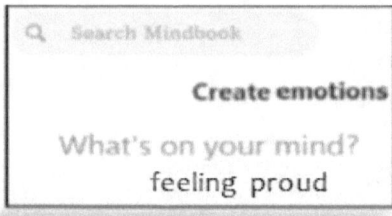

I used to be lost about my work,
Not enjoying anything that I did, much
Then I found my calling
And now 24 hours seem less to do all the work I want to do

I dreamt of writing books and weaving stories,
Thinking of it as an otherworldly thing
Then I began to write
And now I have won not one but multiple awards and accolades for stories that I penned

I used to be an introvert,
Hesitating to take initiative in most things
But now I lean more towards being an ambivert on most days
And am generally game for talking to new people and trying out something new

Can these, be called milestones?
Maybe so
Did they make me proud?
Most definitely so
Would I call one of them my biggest milestone?
I don't think so

Because you see,
I have always been a socially awkward being of sorts
In a crowd if someone singled me out,
I would shy away or just nod my head on their comment about me
But this one time, someone introduced me to the guests as 'Mr.

XXX's wife'
And I said, 'Not XXX's wife, first I'm **Manali Desai**'
I shocked those around
And pleasantly surprised myself as well
I did not apologize about what I said either,
The old me would have
But this time, I was determined
It was definitely a huge milestone crossed

Not taking things lying down
Not allowing someone to belittle me
Not letting myself be defined on their terms
Standing up for what I believe in
Voicing out my thoughts without bothering whether someone will like it or not
THAT
For me was growth
THAT
For me was bigger than any professional achievement or even a personal one
THAT
For me was a milestone to be most proud of

Lost At First Sight

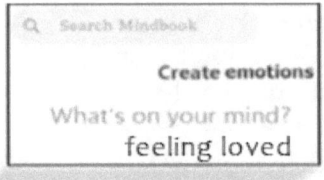

"What would you like to have?"
"A chocolate milkshake, please. Thank you!"

He asked out of chivalry
Wanting to make a good first impression
They were after all, meeting for the first time.
He walked towards the counter, with some clarity on at least two things
"Well, she is a cliche. Chocolate milkshake?"
"I'll be having coffee. Thank you very much for asking!"

She was rather impressed with his initiative
"Let's not get ahead of ourselves here"
She didn't dwell on the date or on **him** much
Her love beckoned,
Crowded cafes or weekends weren't her cup of *anything*
If it were in her hands, she'd have stayed with her beloved in bed
Sighing, she took out her colourful companion
And dove straight into its pages,
Tuning out everything and everyone around her

He stood at the counter, awaiting the order
There was impatience coupled with some excitement
His companion for the evening seemed cute after all
Out of curiosity, he decided to check what she was up to
His eyebrows shot through the roof when he saw her nose dug deep
Lost in the pages, a faint smile on her lips
He felt a gamut of emotions
Anger, for being considered unworthy of her attention
Perplexity, for not understanding the inclination to indulge in

something like this at such a place and time
Lost, about how to navigate the evening from here on

"*Hi, here's your shake*"
She looked up, startled
Lost for a second, trying to find her bearings
Recalling where she was and why she was there
He chuckled and said, "*Glad to have your undivided attention, finally!*"
That's when she noticed the smile
Leaving a dimple on the right chin in its wake
That gave a mischievousness to his face
Adding to the look in his eyes
Full of disbelief and giving her the feeling that he was mocking her
Raising an eyebrow, she thought to herself, "*Hmm, let's give this one a try then*"
And smiled at her companion,
Compelled majorly by that dimple
Which was straight out of the pages she'd been devouring

He noticed her shut the book
With some determination, and maybe a little aggression?
He couldn't be sure
But not one to forget his manners, he smiled
It had a mixed effect, she looked lost for a bit, giving him a peculiar look
But then she smiled, quite disarmingly,
"*Hmm, let's give this one a try then*" he thought while taking the seat opposite her
Compelled by that smile that was still making his heart flutter,
A feeling that had been alien for him as yet

P.S: This poem is inspired by my first meeting with my now husband, Manan Desai

It Might Just Come True

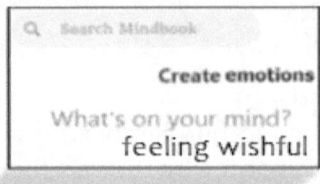

When she was but a child,
She was introduced to a world beyond what she could see,
It was then that she understood the power of words,
She knew she had found her happy place, at long last.

That night, as she lay holding it in her hands,
She looked out the window with dreamy eyes
Maybe she'd already started seeing things that weren't real
But she saw something she'd only heard about or seen in movies

Yes, a shooting star!
She hugged her new friend tight,
For making this possible.
Without preamble, she wished for this friend to be with her always

Lo, and behold
Decades later,
It remains by her side,
Continuing to give her many such precious days and nights

It's true what they say about wishes,
Be careful what you ask for,
Because good or bad,
It might just come true

Can You Help Me Understand?

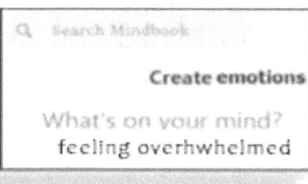

A person's gender,
Becomes a deciding factor,
For their education, career, marriage, family, freedom, choices,
Just about anything they do in life
Can you help me understand?
Why does it matter if someone is he, she, or they, and can't we accept each other as 'humans' first?

A person's sexuality,
Becomes questionable and debatable,
Against nature, religion, culture, and whatnot
Every which way, there's a lack of acceptance
Can you help me understand?
Why does it matter who a person wants to love when we're all actively always seeking and craving for it?

An individual's religion,
Is assumed or asked about,
Before getting to know who they are and what they do,
An assessment and a report card is issued, without any examination
Can you help me understand?
How does which family or region we are born into, make us different from one another?

An individual's decision,
Their life, their choice,
But almost everyone has an opinion
Whether asked or not, most have some advice
Can you help me understand?
How does it matter to so many, when it affects only one or a few?

To all the authors and writers whose writings I've read till date
To all the readers who have read my writings over the years
To all the people who pushed me to write

Thank You

Books by This Author

Under the Mistletoe & Other Stories

Diana is all set to welcome her loved ones for Christmas. An unexpected (and uninvited!) guest shows up at her door, spoiling her festive mood. All her attempts to thwart Dylan's intrusion go in vain as he keeps dropping in, again and again, insisting that she join his family for Christmas Eve dinner. Against her better judgment, she finally gives in, just to get him off her back. As they stand under the mistletoe after the dinner, Diana and Dylan know things have changed for the better for both.

A group of passengers is stranded at the airport together on New Year's Eve. Their plans were to celebrate the last day of the year and then ring in the new year with their loved ones by their side. But a delayed flight mars their plans and their happiness. They end up talking to each other, exchanging their New Year's Eve plans and how they celebrated it these many years so far. As they all welcome the new year together at midnight, their combined resolutions are to stay in touch with each other. They also resolve to make the best out of whatever life throws their way. Because as they have seen and experienced, not all things go as planned, always.

Samantha is visiting her native, Benakatti, after many years. Even though it's Christmas time, it's not a happy occasion in the family. As friends and family drop in for a visit, Samantha recalls the many winter breaks she spent in this village as a child. An unexpected guest shows up one day, bringing forth a cherished memory they had made on a foggy winter day many years ago.

These and 10 other stories encompass this festive special anthology. These are stories of hope, love, healing, new beginnings, acceptance, and everything that the holidays represent.

Love (Try) Angle – Love Trials I

Ayesha has just moved to the' City of Dreams' with her parents. She befriends the charming Viren, who helps her find her footing in Mumbai. Though she is slowly adjusting to her new life, what Ayesha is most excited about is pursuing B.A. (Hons.) Political Science from a reputed college. Things don't go as smoothly as she had thought though. Because Abhi, her senior, seems hell-bent on making her life on the campus difficult from day one. Just when things seem settled, Viren joins the college as an Ad-Hoc lecturer. Is there more to Ayesha's friendship with Viren, and her frenemity with Abhi? It seems there's a love triangle blooming around the corner or will it be a Love (Try) Angle? Because Ayesha is not sure if it's love at all.

Love & (Mellow) Drama - Love Trials II

Gayatri Kulkarni: A Gen-Z girl who has always lived under the shadow of her elder brother Sharad; so much so that she even chose her degree and college following in his footsteps. Although she doesn't regret it, she wishes her parents would understand her dream to pursue her one true passion - DANCE.
Varun Agarwal: A millennial who believes there are no shortcuts in life. He has learned the hard way that being born into a wealthy family comes with more cons than the world would ever understand. She belongs to a Maharashtrian middle-class family from the suburbs. He hails from an affluent family in South Bombay. The only common point between them - being Mumbaikars. How do their paths cross in this city of dreams? Gayatri believes it's because of Abhi Agarwal, Varun's younger brother, who also happens to be her brother's batchmate and close friend. But Varun has harboured a crush on her long before they exchanged hellos and phone numbers. Their story is a meeting of two generations and families, who are poles apart. Is there drama involved? Gayatri is often called a drama queen by those who know her. But after Varun's entry into her life, she's transformed from Miss Melodrama to Miss Mellowed Drama. Find out all about that transition in this much-awaited spin-off from

Manali Desai's debut novel, *Love (Try) Angle, Love & (Mellow) Drama (Love Trials-II)*

The Art of Being Grateful & Other Stories

Aashna receives a mysterious phone call in the middle of the night. The caller is a girl who says she has been kidnapped and will die if Aashna doesn't help her. Before Aashna can get details about the girl and her whereabouts, the phone gets cut off. Who was she and why did her voice sound eerily familiar? Will Aashna be able to help her?

Maanvi's life has always been about making everyone around realize that she is worthy too. From her test grades to her body type, everyone always had a piece of advice to give or some judgement to pass. How does Maanvi get affected by these? Does she manage to prove her worth to the world?

These and six other stories in this collection, cover a range of genres including romance, mystery, horror, thriller and much more. Delve in for a delightful reading journey!

The Untold Stories

Have you wondered about the events that happen around us? Do you think about the kind of lives people we come across everyday lead, and how they came to be what they are today? Our life is our story, but what about those little everyday incidents which create the anecdotes filling up the chapters of our life story? 'The Untold Stories' shares tiny anecdotes from people's everyday routines which go on to make remarkable chapters in their life stories. These anecdotes range from incidents around contemporary social issues and events such as terrorism and environmental imbalance to those circling around relationships.

A Rustic Mind

"We never think about the effects or repercussions of our everyday actions or even the things we come across on daily basis. Through 'A Rustic Mind' I aim to provide a thoughtful take on such actions and incidents. Poetic in its expression, these words will strike a chord which is not only deep but relatable on many levels. "

Ten Tales

This is a collection of short stories by authors across the world. The stories have been handpicked and selected based on their quality. The stories cover all genres in fiction.

Manali's story in this book is titled 'I'm Glad I'm Not Beautiful'. It spins a story around the much needed to be curbed issue and social stigma of acid attacks. The story circles around two school going teenage girls, Abha and Vidhya, who are best friends, but are opposite in nature and appearance and how a few incidents on a particular day turns their lives upside down.

Zista

"Zista represents Culture, the hub of which lies in India."

This title holds in its pages the very essence of India, its people and its culture, conveyed through a selection of short stories by few of the best authors of India.

Manali's story in this book is titled 'The Walls Have Ears'. This story helped her bag the Best Script Award. It talks about a young girl's day out in the infamous Kamathipura aka The Red-Light District of Mumbai.

Petrichor (compiled and edited by Manali Desai)

14 writers
7 short stories
9 poems

Who doesn't hold a special love for the rains? The smell of wet soil when the showers hit the surface of the Earth, opens up so much for us, emotionally. In this magical collection, we have some of the most special monsoon stories from a bunch of talented writers across the world. The contributors of this anthology traverse from 8 years old to 30 years old. What's common between them? Their love for monsoons of course! Because love for the rains is not age bound, right? This anthology is an attempt at bringing together writers from various walks of life. Each story or poem in this collection will make you rekindle your love with this most beloved season. It will be hard not to reminisce about your many romances with Indra over the years. The pages within this book will evoke nostalgic feelings in every reader. So, grab a cup of your favorite beverage and cozy up in your reading nook as you delve into Petrichor.

About the Author

Manali Desai

Manali is a full-time freelance writer and editor cum blogger. Currently, apart from her ad hoc writing and editing assignments, Manali runs a blog and is also a partner with Pachyderm Tales. In her authoring journey, Manali has written and published seven solo books, been a part of a few co-authored books, and has helped new and aspiring writers publish their books as well. She has been a multiple-times bestselling author on Amazon with all her books ranking in the top ten in many categories. Her short story, ***The Walls Have Ears***, helped her bag the **Best Short Story Award in 2019**. She has also won the **Best Author: Fiction Award**, and the **Book of The Year title in 2021** for her debut novel, ***Love (Try) Angle***. Her short story titled, ***The (Un)Blind Date***, which is a part of her Christmas special anthology, ***Under the Mistletoe & Other Stories***, won the best story prize in an online contest, before the book's release in December 2021. ***Mindful Musings & Peaceful Ponderings***, her sixth book, is a poetry anthology based on human emotions. Her latest novel, ***Love & (Mellow) Drama*** is her second long-form fiction book and is a spin-off from her debut novel, ***Love (Try) Angle***.

www.ingramcontent.com/pod-product-compliance
Lightning Source LLC
LaVergne TN
LVHW041628070526
838199LV00052B/3282